SHORT CIRCUI

WALKS

IN

EAST STAFFORDSHIRE

by

John N. Merrill

Maps & photographs by John N. Merrill

FOOTPRINT PRESS Ltd.,
- "from footprint to finished book."

1996

View from Sierra Blanca over White Mountains

FOOTPRINT PRESS Ltd.,
19, Moseley Street, Ripley Derbyshire DE5 3DA
Tel/Fax 01773 - 512143

Email 100777. 2630 @ compuserve.com

Printed, bound, marketed and distributed by Footprint Press Ltd.

© Text and route - Suncrest Ventures Ltd 1996.
@ Maps and photographs - Suncrest Ventures Ltd 1996.

First Published - January 1996

ISBN 1 874754 05 5

U.S.A. office -
Hummingbird Ranch,
Van Horn,
Texas U.S.A.

Please note - The maps in this guide are purely illustrative. You are encouraged to use the appropriate 1:25,000 O.S. map.

Meticulous research has been undertaken to ensure that this publication is highly accurate at the time of going to press. The publishers, however, cannot be held responsible for alterations, errors, omissions, or for changes in details given. They would welcome information to help keep the book up to date.

British Library Cataloguing-in-Publication Data. A catalogue record of this book is available from the British Library.

Typeset in Booksman - bold, italic and plain 10pt and 14pt.

Designed and typset by Suncrest Ventures Ltd.

Cover sketch - "Hanbury " by John Creber - © Suncrest Ventures Ltd. 1996.

About John N. Merrill

John combines the characteristics and strength of a mountain climber with the stamina and athletic capabilities of a marathon runner. In this respect he is unique and has to his credit a whole string of remarkable long walks. He is without question the world's leading marathon walker.

Over the last twenty-five years he has walked more than 160,000 miles and successfully completed more than a dozen walks of a least 1,000 miles or more. His six major walks in Great Britain are -

Hebridean Journey....... 1,003 miles.
Northern Isles Journey......913 miles.
Irish Island Journey ....1,578 miles.
Parkland Journey.......2,043 miles.
Land's End to John o' Groats.....1,608 miles.

and in 1978 he became the first person to walk the entire coastline of Britain - 6,824 miles in ten months.

In Europe he has walked across Austria - 712 miles - hiked the Tour of Mont Blanc, completed High Level Routes in the Dolomites and Italian Alps, walked the Normandy coast, the Sentier de Seine (200 miles) and the Loire Valley (450 miles) in France, and the GR20 route across Corsica in training! Climbed the Tatra Mountains, walked in the Black Forest. and climbed all the highest mountains and skied in Norway 8 times. He has walked across Europe - 2,806 miles in 107 days - crossing seven countries, the Swiss and French Alps and the complete Pyrennean chain - the hardest and longest mountain walk in Europe, with more than 600,000 feet of ascent!

In America he used The Appalachian Trail - 2,200 miles - as a training walk, before walking from Mexico to Canada via the Pacific Crest Trail in record time - 118 days for 2,700 miles. Recently he walked most of the Continental Divide Trail and much of New Mexico; his second home. In Canada he has walked the Rideau Trail - Kingston to Ottowa - 220 miles and The Bruce Trail - Tobermory to Niagara Falls - 460 miles.

John set off from Virginia Beach on the Atlantic coast, and walked 4,226 miles without a rest day, across the width of America to Santa Cruz and San Francisco on the Pacific coast. His walk is unquestionably his greatest achievement, being, in modern history, the longest, hardest crossing of the U.S.A. in the shortest time - under six months (178 days). The direct distance is 2,800 miles.

Between major walks John is out training in his own area - The Peak District National Park. He has walked all of our National Trails many times - The Cleveland Way thirteen times and The Pennine Way four times in a year! He has been trekking in the Himalayas five times. He created more than a dozen challenge walks which have been used to raise more than £500,000 for charity. From his own walks he has raised over £110,000. He is author of more than one hundred and twenty walking guides which he prints and publishes himself, His book sales are in excess of 3 million, He has created many long distance walks including The Limey Way , The Peakland Way, White and Dark Peak Challenge walk, The Rivers' Way, Belvoir Witches Challenge Walk, The Sweet Pea Walk and Middlewich Challenge.

3

CONTENTS

INTRODUCTION

It was while delivering some books to a shop in Tutbury that the owner asked why I had not written about walks in East Staffordshire. He informed me about the story of the Fauld Crater and I made a mental note to look into the area later. I little thought several years would pass before I began exploring the area. I had already walked in the northern area on the Weaver Hills and along the River Dove, but the southern half was totally knew to me.

This book took longer than I planned simply because I ran into many rights of way problems. On one walk alone I came to five different places to find the footpath sign but no stile and no way through the hedge! In the end I scrapped half the walks and started again. I am glad I perservered for the area has much to offer the walker and deserves exploring. The walks take you onto the Weaver Hills and beside the River Dove, on good paths. The Hanbury area is well stiled and has delightful walking. Rocester is fascinating and worth the road walking in places to explore the area. Croxden Abbey is a gem in a delighful location. Kingstone is an unspoilt village with attractive walking. The walk around Blithfield Reservoir is a delight whatever the season. Newborough and Hoar Cross are both fascinating. In the south is Bagot's Wood and the remains of Needwood Forest, which although little walked is peaceful walking. Tutbury has its lofty castle and impressive church while the southern eastern corner has Burton Upon Trent and the Trent & Mersey Canal. Combined the area makes rewarding walking for the local and visitor who want explore quiet and peaceful countryside. I have enjoyed visiting and walking through new and familiar countryside and hope you too discover and enjoy this area of Staffordshire.

Happy walking!
John N. Merrill. 1996

5

ABOUT THE WALKS

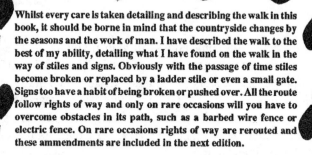

Whilst every care is taken detailing and describing the walk in this book, it should be borne in mind that the countryside changes by the seasons and the work of man. I have described the walk to the best of my ability, detailing what I have found on the walk in the way of stiles and signs. Obviously with the passage of time stiles become broken or replaced by a ladder stile or even a small gate. Signs too have a habit of being broken or pushed over. All the route follow rights of way and only on rare occasions will you have to overcome obstacles in its path, such as a barbed wire fence or electric fence. On rare occasions rights of way are rerouted and these ammendments are included in the next edition.

The seasons bring occasional problems whilst out walking which should also be borne in mind. In the height of summer paths become overgrown and you will have to fight your way through in a few places. In low lying areas the fields are often full of crops, and although the pathline goes straight across it may be more practical to walk round the field edge to get to the next stile or gate. In summer the ground is generally dry but in autumn and winter, especially because of our climate, the surface can be decidedly wet and slippery; sometimes even gluttonous mud!

These comments are part of countryside walking which help to make your walk more interesting or briefly frustrating. Standing in a farmyard up to your ankles in mud might not be funny at the time but upon reflection was one of the highlights of the walk!

The mileage for each walk is based on three calculations -

1. pedometer reading.
2. the route map measured on the map.
3. the time I took for the walk.

I believe the figure stated for each walk to be very accurate but we all walk differently and not always in a straight line! The time allowed for each walk is on the generous side and does not include pub stops etc. The figure is based on the fact that on average a person walks 2 1/2 miles an hours but less in hilly terrain.

The River Dove, near Tutbury.

The Goats Head Inn, Abbot's Bromley.

7

OKEOVER PARK - 5 1/2 MILES

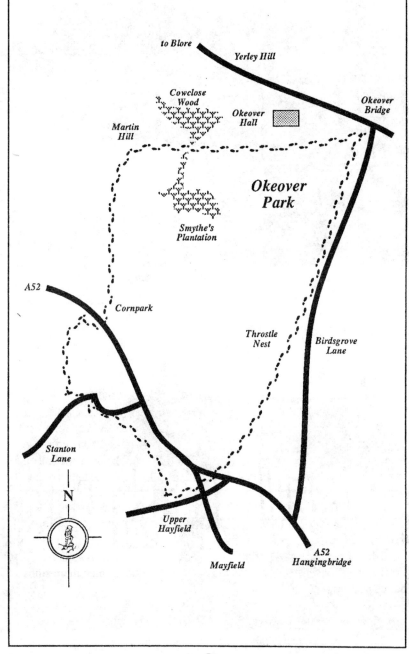

to Blore

Yerley Hill

Cowclose
Wood

Okeover
Hall

Okeover
Bridge

Martin
Hill

Okeover
Park

Smythe's
Plantation

A52

Cornpark

Throstle
Nest

Birdsgrove
Lane

Stanton
Lane

N

Upper
Hayfield

A52
Hangingbridge

Mayfield

OKEOVER PARK
- 5 1/2 MILES
- allow 2 hours.

 - Okeover Bridge - Okeover Park - Martin Hill - Cornpark - Stanton Lane - Upper Hayfield - Throstle Nest - Okeover Bridge.

 1:25,000 Pathfinder Series Sheet No. SK 04/14 - Ashbourne and the Churnet Valley.

- None.

None. Nearest - Okeover Arms in Mapleton,Derbyshire.

ABOUT THE WALK - The walk uses little used rights of way through Okeover Park to Upper Hayfield. The scenery is outstanding and the views of Okeover Hall are attractive. There is no car park, with only limited road parking near Okeover Bridge and Mapleton. The walk overlooks the Peak District and lies in the north- eastern corner of East Staffordshire.

WALKING INSTRUCTIONS - Cross Okeover Bridge over the River Dove, which is also the boundary between Derbyshire and Staffordshire. Walk along the road to the road on your left - Birdsgrove Lane - through Okeover Park and opposite Okeover Mill. Turn left along the road for a few yards and before the road junction to Okeover Hall, turn right and cross the road and aim for the righthand side of a shallow dale. Ascend with the hall on your right, following a faint path. Pass a solitary oak and 1/4 mile later a ruined farm and continue to a metal ladder stile at the junction of two plantations. Cross the stile and keep the wood on your left before crossing the field towards the farm, Martin Hill, reached via a stile and walled track. At the farm turn left along a track and where it turns right keep ahead to a gate. Continue to the immediate righthand side of Lower Grounds Farm, where there is a stile. Keep the field edge (hedge) on your right and you will come to three more stiles before bearing right to the A52 road near Cornpark.

Turn right and just past a layby is a footpath sign, on the right of a house. Turn left and keep to the righthand side of the narrow field to a stile on the lefthand side. Cross to another and bear slightly left to a gate and hedged track. Go through this and follow the hedged track round to your left to a stile on your right. Aim towards the righthand corner of the field where there is a gate. Go through and keep the hedge on your right and descend to Stanton Lane. Turn left and in 1/4 mile on your right is a gate by an oak tree. Cross the field to a stile and bear left aiming for the far righthand corner of the field. Before you get there, go through a stile on your right, and descend with the field edge on your left, to a stile and onto the lane at Upper Hayfield. Turn left and walk through the village, keeping straight ahead at the cross roads and reach the A52 road.

Turn right then left down a track which soon turns right down to a ruined farm building. Keep to the righthand side of the field coming to gates and stiles to reach the farm road to Throstle Nest. Cross over and aim for the righthand corner of the field to a gate and Birdsgrove Lane. Turn left and walk along the lane through Okeover Park back to your start.

OKEOVER HALL - In 1150 the Abbot of Burton, granted the lands of Okeover to Ralph Fitzormos De Okeover. A descendant of the female line, Sir Ian Walker Okeover, the third baronet lives here today. The Palladian building is the work of Leake Okeover - 1701 - 1765. In the 19th century it was altered and in 1960 enlarged. The wrought iron entrance gates were made by Robert Bakewell, the well known Derby ironsmith in the 18th. century.

Okeover Hall.

The Cock Inn, Hanbury - Hanbury walks.

Churnet Bridge and River Churnet at Rocester - Rocester walk.

STANTON & THE WEAVER HILLS
- 6 MILES

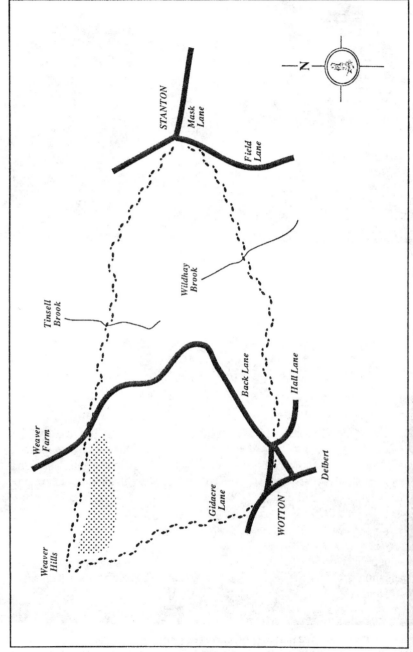

STANTON

Mask Lane

Field Lane

Wildhay Brook

Tinsell Brook

Back Lane

Hall Lane

Weaver Farm

Gidacre Lane

Delbert

WOTTON

Weaver Hills

STANTON & THE WEAVER HILLS
- 6 MILES
- allow 2 1/2 hours.

- Stanton - Wildhay Brook - Wootton - Gidacre Lane - Weaver Hills - Tinsell Brook - Stanton.

 1:25,000 Pathfinder Series Sheet No. SK 04/14 - Ashbourne and the Churnet Valley.

- None. Roadside parking in Stanton.

- None.

ABOUT THE WALK - The Weaver Hills are one of the finest viewpoints in Staffordshire and on a clear day six counties can be seen. You start from and pass through attractive villages before the ascent. Most of the route follows little used rights of way but all the stiles and signs are there. The first 1/4 mile of the route you, you return on.

WALKING INSTRUCTIONS - Starting from the southern side of Stanton at the junction of Mask Lane and Field Lane - the road to Ellastone. Turn left down this road to a chapel on your left. Opposite on your right is a stile. Go through here and descend the field to a stile and ascend via steps to a stile with a house on your left. You return to this point on your way back. Through the stile turn left and walk along the lefthand side of the field to a gate. Through this reach a stile on your right then bear left down the righthand side of the field to a stile. Through this bear left and descend to a stile. Descend steeply to your right to Wildhay Brook, to a stile and footbridge - this section of the route is little used. Ascend steeply the other side with a wall/fence on your left. At the top is a gate. Bear left beyond and cross the field to a stile. Keep the hedge on your right to another stile and continue basically straight ahead passing a well and more stiles to reach Hall Lane in Wootton, via a stile beside a path sign - *"Stanton."*

Turn right up the lane and keep straight ahead through the village past "Rock Cottage - 1670", to the main road. Keep straight ahead along it for a few

Kevin quarry.

yards to the first track on your right - Gidacre Lane; signed Wootton Cricket Club. Walk up the track and pass the cricket field on your left and continue across a field to a gate; ahead can be seen the Weaver Hills. Now start angling up to your right, first to a stile and then more steeply to another, aiming for the righthand side of the saddle between the hills. Below to your left is Kevin Quarry. Continue ascending to another stile and wall on level ground. Continue beyond to a track and wall; on your left is the summit of the hills, 371 metres. Turn right and keep the wall on your left, then right to reach the road 1/2 mile away. Turn right and before the cattle grid turn left at a stile and path sign. Descend the field to a gate and bear right passing a limestone knoll on your left. Continue descending to a stile and on down to a stile and stepping stones over Tinsell Brook. Bear right passing a pond on your right to another stile - now back in gritstone country. keep ahead along the field boundaries guided by stiles and in 1/2 mile reach the house and stile you walked past at the start. Descend the steps and retrace your steps back to Field Lane and chapel and turn left back into Stanton village. An exceptional walk on little used paths through a very attractive area.

Croxden Abbey - Croxden walk.

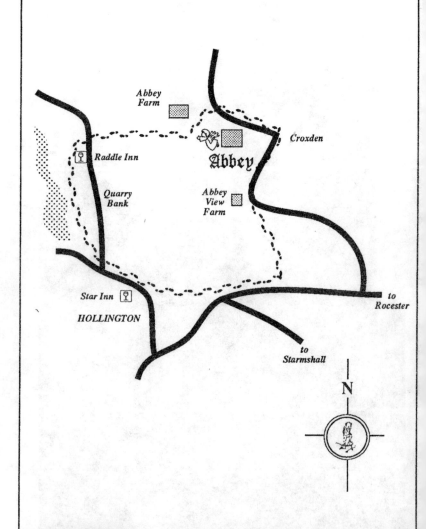

CROXDEN ABBEY - Founded by Bertram de Verdun who also started Alton Castle, in the 12th century. Most of the ruins date from the 13th century and the walls of the west front are 40 feet high. The remains of the cloisters, south transept, sacristy and 14th century guest house can be seen. In the 14th century a monk, William de Shepesheved, wrote a Chronicle of the Abbey, and this is now in the British Museum.

HOLLINGTON & CROXDEN ABBEY - 3 MILES
- allow 2 hours.

-Hollington - Butterley Bank - Croxden - Croxden Abbey - Quarry Bank - Hollington.

 1:25,000 Pathfinder Series Sheet No. 831 (SK 03/13) - Uttoxeter.

 - None. Roadside parking only.

- The Raddle Inn, Quarry Bank, Hollington. Star Inn, Hollington.

ABOUT THE WALK - A short but beautiful one to see the impressive ruins of Croxden Abbey; a jewel of East Staffordshire! Parking is limited and the rights of way are little used.

WALKING INSTRUCTIONS - Starting from Hollington walk down the road past the Star Inn, and just after where the road turns right is a stile on your left. Turn left and descend to another stile. Keep the field edge on your right and continue descending to a gate and road. Turn left along the road towards Butterley Bank Farm, but before the farm - approx. 1/4 mile of road walking - is a stile and footpath sign on your left. Turn left and basically keep straight ahead to reach the stiles and in a 1/3 mile reach the road beside Abbey View Farm, via a stile beside a path sign. Turn left and follow the road round into Croxden and round to your left to the Abbey. Just past the Abbey turn left past Abbey Farm and bear right past it before turning left at a stone stile. Cross Croxden Brook keeping to the lefthand side of the field to reach a stile. Turn right keeping the hedge on your left to another stile. Now keep the hedge on your right and reach a gate. Through this bear slightly left to pass a boundary stone - CR/CH. Just after is a stone stile and beyond a track. Turn left up the track to Quarry Bank and the Raddle Inn. Turn right and just past the inn turn left at a stile and ascend the path to another stile. Just after reach a track and turn left along it through the trees and past old quarries to the road junction with Quarry Bank. Turn left (not sharp left) and descend back into Hollington and the Star Inn.

ROCESTER & RIVER DOVE
- 5 1/2 MILES

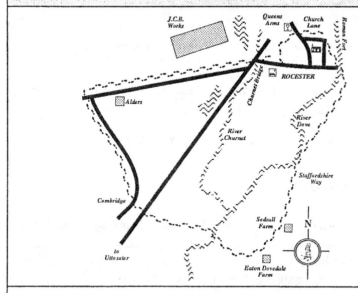

from opposite page - right, first to a foot-bridge and then onto stiles. You leave the riverside as it takes a large meander and aim towards the wooded base of the hills at Sedsall Rough. Here you rejoin the river momentarily before continuing along the base of the hills guided by stiles and a track to Sedsall Farm and onto Eaton Dovedale Farm. Here the Staffordshire Way sign states - Rocester/Uttoxeter. Here you leave the "Way" and head west-wards along the farm track to the River Dove and new road.

Cross the new road and follow the lane beyond to Combridge and Combridge Farm. Pass The Tyke and farm on your left and follow the lane past Cornhill Farm and cross a ford via a footbridge. There are two rights of way to your right, but they are impracticable to use. Continue to the road junction and turn right and follow the road back to Rocester, little over a mile away. In 3/4 mile pass the JCB works on your left and lakes on your right. Cross the road into Rocester over the Churnet Bridge back to your start.

ROCESTER - The abbey was founded in 1146 and apart from some mounds little remains. The Roman Fort covered seven acres. The church, dedicated to St. Michael, was restored in 1873. Inside is an attractive window showing ten scenes of Christ's life, pained by Mr. De Morgan. In the churchyard is a 700 years old cross shaft, the finest in Staffordshire and England. JCB was founded in 1949 and the works is on the site of the Rocester Cheese Factory.

18

ROCESTER
& RIVER DOVE
- 5 1/2 MILES
- allow 2 hours.

- -- -- -- *Rocester - Churnet Bridge - Rocester Bridge - Staffordshire Way - River Dove - Eaton Dovedale Farm - Combridge - Alders - JCB Plant - Rocester.*

 - 1;25,000 Pathfinder Series Sheet No. 831 (SK 03/13) - Uttoxeter.

*near Churnet Bridge.*

- Queens Arms, Rocester.

ABOUT THE WALK - Rocester is a delightful unspoilt village with the site of a Roman Fort and Abbey on its eastern edge. The walk takes around the village before joining the Staffordshire Way, which you follow for 1 1/2 miles to Eaton Dovedale Farm. From here you cross the River Dove, close its confluence with the River Churnet and step back into Staffordshire; having been in Derbyshire for the last mile. Soon afterwards you cross the new road and follow lanes and minor roads back to Rocester, passing the JCB complex with lakes and Nature Reserve. There are rights of way across the fields but there is no stiles or signs, so you have no alternative but to road walk.

WALKING INSTRUCTIONS - From the car park return to the road and turn left and just before the Churnet Bridge, turn right, as footpath signed, and walk beside the River Churnet for a short distance. At the end of the field turn right along the field boundary to reach the houses of Rocester and the Queen Arms Inn. Cross the road and continue ahead along Church Lane. In 1/4 mile the lane turns left, with St. Michael's church on your right and First Dove School on your left. Continue ahead a short distance before turning right along the edge, passing some cottages on your left. You are now on the Staffordshire Way. To your left is the site of the Abbey and beyond the Roman Fort. Gaining the road turn left passing Arkwright's Mill dated 1781/2 on your left. 100 yards later cross Rocester Bridge over the River Dove and turn right - following the Staffordshire Way. For the next 1/2 mile you keep close to the river on your

CALWICH ABBEY
AND RIVER DOVE - 4 1/2 MILES

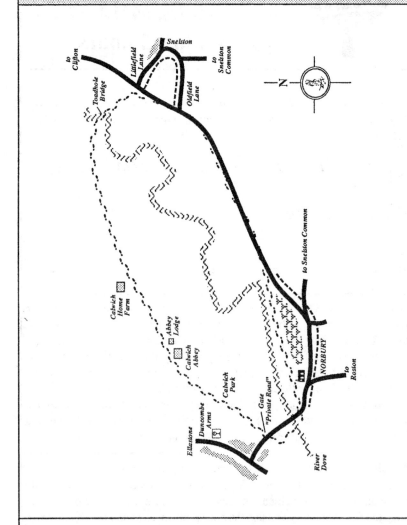

From opposite page - At the road turn right and follow it for 3/4 mile. Pass a couple of cottages on your right and Norbury sign on your left. 30 yards later turn right into the pine trees and follow the path above the river for 1/2 mile to a stile and footbridge over a mill leat, with a weir on your right. Ascend another stile beyond before following the banks of the Dove to your right to the road bridge where you started. To visit Norbury Church instead of walking through the pine trees, continue on the road, turning right at all junctions. The church is signed on your right.

CALWICH ABBEY
AND RIVER DOVE
- 4 1/2 MILES
- allow 2 hours.

River Dove - Calwich Park - Calwich Abbey - Toad Hole Bridge - Snelston - Norbury - River Dove.

 - 1:25,000 Pathfinder Series Sheet No. SK 04/14 - Ashbourne and the Churnet Valley.

 *No official car park.*

No inn on the walk, Duncombe Arms in Ellastone.

ABOUT THE WALK - a very pleasant walk up the Dove valley, through Calwich Park and impressive mansion to the Toadhole footbridge over the Dove. Upon reaching the road a 3/4 mile extension will bring you into the attractive village of Snelston. The final part of the walk is beside the Dove and through pine forest. A visit to Norbury Church is particularly interesting to see the Fitzherberts' memorials and hall.

WALKING INSTRUCTIONS - Starting from the road bridge over the River Dove, midway between Norbury and Ellastone, follow the road towards Lower Ellastone. Just where you enter, turn right to a gate and drive - Private Road. This is the footpath through Calwich Park. The drive is well fenced. Simply keep ahead to the next gate where you enter open country. 1/2 mile later gain the gate with the impressive stable block of Calwich Abbey beyond. Follow the track first to your left then right past Abbey Lodge. Continue on the drive over the cattle grid to the next one. 1/2 mile later, close to Calwich Home Farm. Cross another shortly afterwards and turn right down the track. Where it enters a private house descend to your left to a stile pass the rock escarpment to the river plain and a stile and footbridge, Cross the next field to the River Dove and prominent Toadhole Foot Bridge, Follow the stiled track beyond to the road. You now follow the road to your right for 3/4 mile, but by crossing over and following - Littlefield Lane - you can explore the village of Snelston. In the village turn right, then right again onto - Oldfield Lane - and this will return you to the Norbury road.

KINGSTONE - 4 MILES

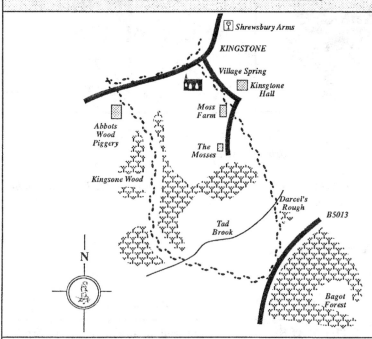

Shrewsbury Arms, Kingstone.

from opposite page - of Kingstone church. You are now following a track to a lane close to The Mosses. Go through the gate and follow the lane - Church Lane - past Moss Farm and Kingstone Hall. Soon afterwards pass on your left the village spring and church. Turn right back to the inn.

KINGSTONE
- 4 MILES
- allow 1 1/2 hours.

•• •• •• •• *Kingstone - Kingstone Wood - B5013 - Bagot Forest - Darcel's Rough - The Mosses - Kingstone Hall - Kingstone.*

O.S. MAP - *1:25,000 Pathfinder Series Sheet No. SK 02/12 - Abbots Bromley.*

P - *None. Roadside parking only.*

- *Shrewsbury Arms, Kingstone.*

ABOUT THE WALK - Kingstone is tucked out of the way and deserves a visit! An attractive village which has won the best village award. The church stands above the stream and is reached via a footbridge. Closeby is the village spring used by the villagers for water until 1936. The walk takes you on good paths through woodland and beside Bagot Forest.

WALKING INSTRUCTIONS - From the Shrewsbury Arms walk down the road towards the church. On your left is Church Lane, which is your return route. Continue along the road for nearly 1/2 mile to the first farm drive on your left. Turn left past Abbots Wood Piggery to a gate, following a bridlepath. Continue ahead beside the fence on your left to a gate and Kingstone Wood. Continue ahead through the wood following the path which curves right to a junction of tracks. Here keep straight ahead and soon come to the righthand edge of the wood before walking through the middle of it to a gate at its southern edge. Continue to a gate and cross Tad Brook. Keep to the righthand side of the field to another gate and pond beyond. Continue on the righthand side and in 1/4 mile reach the junction of bridlepaths. Keep straight ahead on a hedged track which brings you to a gate and the B5013 road.

Turn left along the road and follow it for 1/4 mile, with Bagot Forest on your right. At the second field boundary on your left at spot height 124 metres, leave the road and cross diagonally to your right across the field to a stile on the lefthand side of Darcel's Rough. Cross the footbridge over Tad Brook and bear right then left to a gate on the eastern edge of Kingstone Wood. Keep the wood on your left as you curve round to your left and get your first sight of the spire

BAGOT'S PARK - 5 MILES

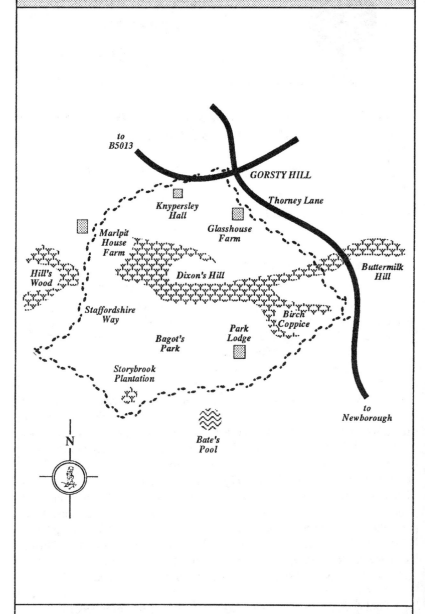

from opposite page - woodland to a stile. Over this descend the field to a stile and footbridge over the brook. Keep to the righthand side of the field to a stile in the far righthand corner, and bear right to a gate close to Glasshouse Farm and Thorney Lane. Turn left up the lane back to the cross roads at Gorsty Hill.

BAGOT'S PARK - 5 MILES
- allow 2 hours.

Gorsty Hill - Knypersley Hall - Marlpit House Farm - Staffordshire Way - Bagot's Park - Bates Pool - Park Lodge - Birch Coppice - Buttermilk Hill - Glasshouse Farm - Gorsty Hill.

 - 1:25,000 Pathfinder Series Sheet No.SK 02/12 - Abbots Bromley.

 None. Roadside parking only.

 none! Carry what you need.

ABOUT THE WALK - This short walk explores a little walked area north of Abbot's Bromley, which deserves exploring! The route follows good paths and tracks past woodland and "parkland".

WALKING INSTRUCTIONS - Starting from the cross-roads at Gorsty Hill turn left (westwards) along the road; the road ahead of you - Thorney Lane - is your return route. Follow the road for a few yards and turn left along the drive past Knypersley Hall to a gate. You are now on a footpath and basically keep ahead and walk round a pond on your right to a stile in the righthand corner of the field. Bear slightly left towards Marlpit House Farm to a gate and track. Here join the Staffordshire Way, which you now follow for the next 1 1/2 miles. Walk along the track to the edge of Hill's Wood on your right, to a stile and footpath sign. Continue across the field to another stile and footpath sign. To your left is a trig point 160m. the highest point on the walk. At the stile bear right slightly continuing on a track and in 1/4 mile pass woodland on your left and reach another stile and path sign. Here turn sharp left to a stile with Story Brook on your left. Continue beside the brook on your left to two more stiles. At the second turn left (leaving the Staffordshire Way) and pass Storybrook Plantation on your left and now walking along a concrete driveway. To your left is New Pool in Bagot's Park. Continue for 3/4 mile and just past Park Lodge on your left reach a gate. Here turn left continuing on the track to a cattle grid and Birch Coppice on your left. At its eastern end, leave the track and cross to the woods edge and gate. Cross the next field keeping to the righthand side, before descending slightly to a stile and woodland. Ascend Buttermilk Hill and

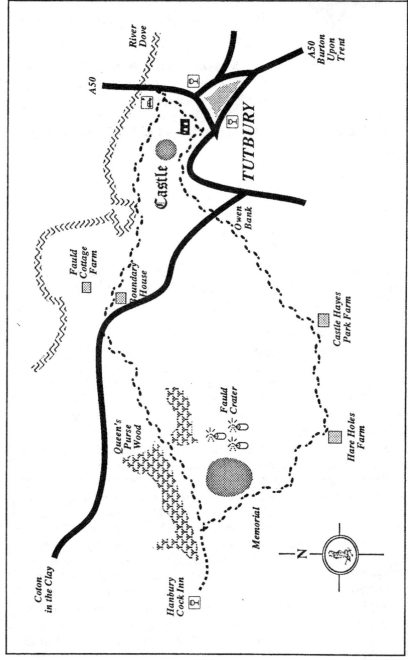

TUTBURY
& HANBURY
- 7 MILES
- allow 3 hours.

- *Tutbury Mill Car Park - River Dove - Fauld Cottage Farm - Stonepit Hills - Fauld Crater - Hare Holes Farm - Castle Hayes Park Farm - Owens Bank - Castle Street - Tutbury - Mill Car Park.*
- *can be extended 1 mile to Hanbury for the Cock Inn and 2 mile walk over Rough Hays.*

 1:25,000 Pathfinder Series Sheet nos.
- *SK 22/32 - Burton Upon Trent.*
- *SK 02/12 - Abbots Bromley.*

 - Tutbury Mill picnic site just off the A50. Grid Ref. SK214294.

- Several in Tutbury including the Ye Olde Dog and Partridge Hotel in the High Street. Just off the route in Hanbury, The Cock Inn.

ABOUT THE WALK - There is much to see on this walk and a full day could be had exploring Hanbury and the Fauld Crater with a visit to Tutbury Castle and church. The paths are defined and the walk can be extended to explore Hanbury more. A very interesting walk with views to the Peakland Hills.

WALKING INSTRUCTIONS - Turn right out of the car park along the track and pass the cricket field on your left. Just after bear left to walk close to the Mill Fleam, with Tutbury Castle above, to a footbridge over the junction of the Fleam and River Dove, 1/2 mile away. Turn left over the bridge and walk along the banks of the river for a 1/3 mile to a ruined building. Here leave the river as it curves right, and keep ahead to a stile in the lefthand corner of the field ahead. Keep to the lefthand side of the field with Fauld Cottage Farm to your right. In 1/3 mile reach the minor road beside Boundary House. Turn right and in a few yards turn left on a road into an industrial estate. Keep straight ahead to the British Gas compound. Here as signed turn right along a field to another stile. Turn left and ascend the lefthand side of the field to a stile and

27

footpath sign. Ascend more steeply with the fence on your left onto Stonepit Hills. The path soon becomes a track as you pass a pheasant enclosure on your left and enter woodland. Where the track divides keep to the lefthand one and basically straight ahead as you gently ascend through woodland to a kissing gate at Brown's Coppice, little over 1/4 mile away. If you keep straight ahead here you can follow the path to Hanbury village 1/2 mile away.

Turn left on the track and soon you pass the Fauld Crater on your left. On your right you will come to a monument to the people who died here. Follow the path around the perimeter of the crater, taking the second signed path on your right. The defined path crosses the field to a gap and continue ahead with the field boundary on your right to reach two stiles with Hare Holes Farm on your right. Go through a stile and onto another keeping to the lefthand side of the field and soon pick up a track to Castle Hayes Park Farm. Walk past the farm on its lefthand side to a stile and continue ahead across the field and after two fields keep the hedge on your right to a stile. After this the hedge is on your left to another stile. Here turn right and ascend with the hedge on your right to the top of the field. Turn left along the lefthand side of the field and where the path divides turn left and keep to the righthand side of the field to a minor road at Owen's Bank. Ahead can be seen Tutbury Castle. Cross the road, as signed, and continue ahead to a stile. Here start angling right across the slope aiming for the top righthand corner close to the castle. Turn right and ascend the steps to the road. Turn left along Castle Street and in a few yards turn left and walk round past the entrance to the castle and onto the church. Continue through the churchyard back to the road and turn left and descend back to car park at the mill site. Where you descend to your right is High Street and the famous Dog and Partridge Hotel.

TUTBURY - The Dog & Partridge Hotel dates from the 14th century when it was a town house of the Curzon family. Later it became a coaching inn. The Priory church dedicated to St. Mary the Virgin, was founded in 1089 and has a most impressive Norman west doorway. Tutbury Castle dates from Norman times and since 1265 has been part of the Duchy of Lancaster. In the 1580's the ill-fated Mary Queen of Scots was "imprisoned" here. King Charles 1st. took refuge here after the Battle of Naseby and was the last royal to stay here.

Tutbury Castle from Mill Fleam.

Monument.

FAULD CRATER - The area is rich in gypsum and alabaster and the Stonepit Hills were mined for it. During the second world war the underground passageways were used to store bombs for the R.A.F. On November 27th 1944 at 11.0a.m. the site blew up creating todays crater and the largest explosion ever of conventional weapons. Tragically buildings disappeared, livestock were swallow up and seventy people died; some were never found. The monument records the names who perished on that fateful day. 4,000 tons exploded creating a crater 12 acres in size and upto 400 feet deep. The explosion was heard in London and in Geneva it was recorded as an earthquake! The Cock Inn has photographs of the crater.

Fauld crater.

HANBURY & COTON IN THE CLAY - 2 MILES

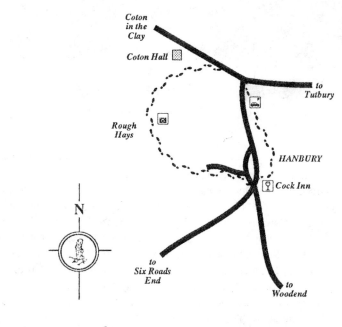

Coton
in the
Clay

Coton Hall

Rough
Hays

to
Tutbury

HANBURY

Cock Inn

N

to
Six Roads
End

to
Woodend

ST.WERBURGH'S CHURCH, HANBURY - Dates from Norman times. Inside are numerous tombs to many leading Staffordshire families. The alabaster tomb to the knight, Sir John Hanbury, who died in 1303 is believed to be the oldest in England. Another is to Ralph Adderley who died in 1595 and his tomb shows his two wives and fifteen children. Near the alter is the 16th century monument to Sir Charles Egerton, an axe bearer in Needwood Forest.

HANBURY & COTON
IN THE CLAY
- 2 MILES
- allow 1 hour.

 *- Hanbury Common - Hanbury - Rough Hays - Coton Road - Hanbury Common.*

 1:25,000 Pathfinder Series Sheet No. SK 02/12 - Abbots Bromley.

- Hanbury Common. Grid Ref. SK 174284.

⟨Y⟩*- The Cock Inn, Hanbury.*

ABOUT THE WALK - A short walk from Hanbury that can be added to others in book or as a walk on its own. The view from Rough Hays is outstanding, across to the Peakland hills. Hanbury is a most attractive village the church and adjacent thatched cottage are a most picturesque setting.

WALKING INSTRUCTIONS - Starting from the car park on Hanbury Hill, at Hanbury Common just to the north of the village. Ascend the path at the back of the car park and follow it towards the village - the path is defined. Reach the road and village and keep to the lefthand road to pass the Cock Inn and the start of the Hanbury Walks. Follow the road round to your right past the Old Forge and bear right on the minor road. Where it turns right keep left on Hall Lane to pass St. Werburgh's church and thatched cottage on your left. Continue down the track to a stile and path sign on your right. Turn right and follow the path across the field, aiming for the righthand side of Rough Hays. Here the view unfolds. Gain a stile and descend the righthand side of the field to a stile by an oak tree. Continue descending to the bottom righthand corner of the field to a gate and track; ahead can be seen the white painted Coton Hall. Turn right along the track to a stile and track to your left to Coton Hall Farm. Go over the stile and gently descend the field to its bottom righthand corner to a stile - as I approached the stile a cow gave birth! Over the wooden stile reach a gate by a path sign and turn right along the road. In a few yards turn right up Hanbury Hill and the car park is 1/4 mile ahead on your left.

HANBURY, FAULD CRATER & GREAVES WOOD - 5 1/2 MILES

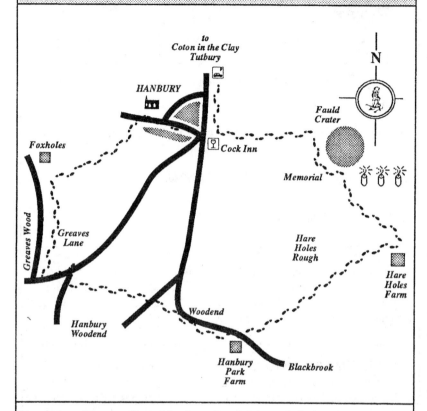

From opposite page - Turn right along the road through the hamlet of Woodend and in little over 1/4 mile at Villa Cottage is a stile on your left. Over this cross the field to another stile beside an oak tree. A few more yards reach another and a minor road. Cross over to a stile and keep to the edge of the field to a stile. Bear slightly left to a gate and footpath sign. Keep to the lefthand edge of the field, beside the hedge to a stile and onto a gate before a minor lane; ahead is Howitt House. Turn right then left along the road towards Six Roads End. In 100 yards turn right and ascend Greaves Lane with Greaves Wood on your left. At the top where the road turns sharp left, turn right, as footpath signed at Foxholes. In a few yards reach a stile on your left. Cross diagonally to another and continue ahead aiming for the righthand side of a small wood. Continue beyond to the field boundary and path sign. Turn left to a stile and Hall Lane. Turn right and walk through the village of Hanbury past the church to the road. You can turn left here and return to the car park, or by bearing right then left return to the Cock Inn; from here retrace your steps back to the car park.

HANBURY, FAULD CRATER & GREAVES WOOD - 5 1/2 MILES - allow 2 or more hours.

➤ *Hanbury - Fauld Crater - Hare Holes Farm - Hare Holes Rough - Hanbury Park Farm - Woodend - Western Cottages - Greaves Wood - Foxholes - Hanbury.*

 - 1:25,000 Pathfinder Series Sheet No. 02/12 - Abbots Bromley.

Just north of the village at Hanbury Common Picnic site. Grid Ref. SK 174284.

- Cock Inn, Hanbury.

ABOUT THE WALK - A walk around the countryside to the south of Hanbury village. First visiting the Fauld Crater before crossing farmland to Woodend. A short road walk brings you to footpaths to Greaves Wood and the return back to Hanbury. The route follows little used rights of way but all the stiles and gates are there. *The walk can be extended by walking the Hanbury/Coton in the Clay route - 2 miles.*

WALKING INSTRUCTIONS - From the car park turn left and ascend the lane - Hanbury Hill - to the village and Cock Inn. Just after turn left, as footpath signed, and go over the stile. Keep beside the field edge to the next stile. Over this Brown's Coppice is on your left and continue to another stile. Ahead is another and over this turn right through the kissing gate. In a few yards on your left can be seen the Fauld Crater. Follow then track/path past the memorial on your right and in 40 yards turn right to a stile and footpath sign. The path line is faint but keep to the righthand side of the field to near Hare Holes Rough and turn left - following marker posts. Cross over the brow of the field to a field boundary, which you keep on your right to a stile and onto another just before Hare Holes Farm. Here turn right and cross the field to a stile. Ahead is another on the corner of woodland. Keep the woodland on your right as you walk along the edge of the field and onto a pond on your right. Cross the southern edge of Hare Holes Rough with stiles and footbridge. Continue straight ahead to a gate and onto another beside a path sign - Tutbury 2 miles - opposite Needwood House.

BLITHFIELD RESERVOIR - 6 MILES

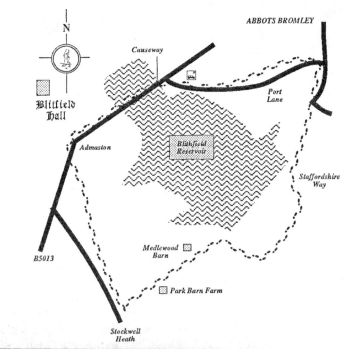

BLITHFIELD HALL
- Home of the Bagot family for nearly 900 years. The world renowned Abbots Bromley Horn Dance is performed in September.

STAFFORDSHIRE WAY
- 92 miles from Mow Cop to Kinver Edge.

BLITHFIELD RESERVOIR
- 6 MILES
- allow 2 1/2 hours.

Blithfield Reservoir - Causeway - Admaston - Stockwell Heath - Staffordshire Way - Park Barn Farm - Medlewood Barn - Staffordshire Way - Port Lane - Blithfield Reservoir.

 - 1:25,000 Pathfinder Series Sheet No. SK 02/12 - Abbots Bromley.

- Just off the Causeway, overlooking the reservoir. Grid Ref. 063239.

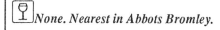*None. Nearest in Abbots Bromley.*

ABOUT THE WALK - A walk encircling the southern end of Blithfield Reservoir, including a section of the Staffordshire Way. The paths are defined and stiled with extensive views over the reservoir.

WALKING INSTRUCTIONS - From the car park return to the main road and turn left and cross the Causeway and onto Admaston a mile away. Walk through the village and opposite the entrance gates to Blithfield Hall is a stile and path sign on your left. Turn left and cross the field to your right to another stile. Continue ahead aiming to for the righthand side of Round Plantation, where there are stiles. Continue across the field to a stile by an oak tree and cross another field to a road and path sign. Turn left along the road to Stockwell Heath. Approaching the village turn left along the road towards Park Barn Farm; you are now on the Staffordshire Way, which is well signed. Walk along the road and as signed leave it to walk beside it on your right, past Park Barn Farm. Continue beside the embankment - Park Vale - to a stile. Follow it round to your right to another stile. Here leave it and turn left along the field edge to Medlewood Barn. Continue ahead towards the dam end of the reservoir and turn right, as signed (Staffordshire Way.) Gain another stile and track and walk along this to a stile on your left. Turn left along the righthand side of the field to a stile and after this one bear left to a track before the river overflow. Turn right along the track and follow it round to just beyond the dam end to a stile on your left. Turn left and soon bear right, following the Staffordshire Way to a T junction. Here leave the Staffordshire Way and turn left along the road. In 1/4 mile keep left and follow the road - Port Lane - all the way back to the car park nearly a mile away.

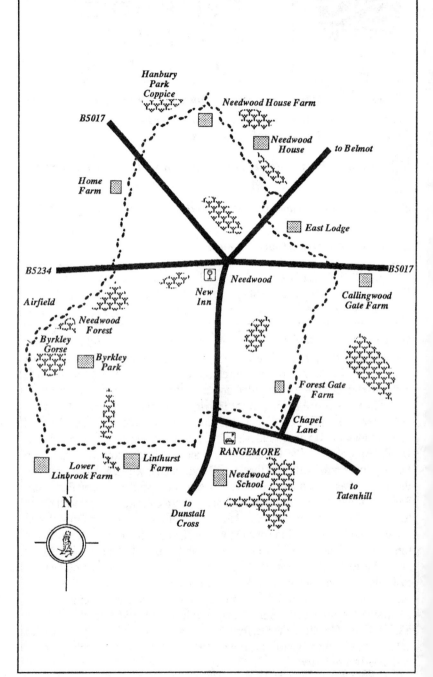

Hanbury
Park
Coppice

Needwood House Farm

B5017

Needwood
House

to Belmot

Home
Farm

East Lodge

B5234

B5017

Needwood

New
Inn

Callingwood
Gate Farm

Airfield

Needwood
Forest

Byrkley
Gorse

Byrkley
Park

Forest Gate
Farm

Chapel
Lane

RANGEMORE

Lower
Linbrook Farm

Linthurst
Farm

Needwood
School

to
Tatenhill

N

to
Dunstall
Cross

NEEDWOOD FOREST
- 7 1/2 MILES
- allow 3 hours.

➡ Rangemore - Forest Gate Farm - B5017 - East Lodge -
Needwood House - Hanbury Park Gate - B5013 - Home Farm - B5234 -
Needwood Forest - Byrkley Gorse - Lower Linbrook Farm - Rangemore.

 - 1:25,000 Pathfinder Series Sheet No. 02/12 - Abbots Bromley.

 - Beside Village Hall in Rangemore.

- None actually on the route. Nearest, 1/4 mile south of East Lodge, at
Needwood - New Inn.

ABOUT THE WALK - A walk around the remnants of Needwood Forest following little used paths. All the stiles and path signs are there.

WALKING INSTRUCTIONS - Starting from All Saints church in Rangemore, turn right along the road for a few yards before turning left along Chapel Lane. At the end of the lane is a stile. Continue ahead to another and keep straight ahead to a gate. Cross the next field to a gate; to your left is the woodland of Holly Bank. Continue slightly right to the far righthand corner of the field, where there is a gap. Beyond pick up a track leading to a gate before gaining the B5017 road at a stile and footpath sign - Rangemore 1/2 mile. On your right is Callingwood Gate Farm. Half mile to your left is the New Inn, at Needwood. Cross the road to a stile and bear half left to a stile and footbridge. Continue ahead to a gap in the field boundary and onto a stile and footbridge; to your left is Paradise Farm. Bear slightly right to East Lodge and turn left beside the wall, and keeping this on your right to reach a stile and road - 1/4 mile to your left is the New Inn.

Turn right and in a few yards, as footpath signed turn left along the tarmaced drive past Needwood House and onto Needwood House Farm. At the end of the buildings turn left along a track through Hanbury Park Coppice. At the end turn left at Hanbury Park Gate and follow the tarmaced surface to the B5012 road.

Go straight across on the track to Home Farm. On your right is a fishing pond. At the end of the buildings gain a gate and keep the hedge on your right and in 1/4 mile reach the B5234 road via a gate. On your right is a popular motor cross field. Cross the road to a gate and continue ahead on a grass track to a stile before Needwood Forest and Byrkley Park. To your right is an airfield. Bear right and keep to the edge of the woodland for 1/2 mile to a stile at the western corner of the woodland, at Byrkley Gorse. Turn left to a stile and keep the hedge on your left to a gate. You now walk along a track to a stile and onto Lower Linbrook Farm. Just before the farm turn left to a stile and onto another. Cross the field to the far lefthand to a stile, footbridge and woodland. Go straight across the woodland to a stile on the otherside. Cross the corner of the field to a stile and walk along the righthand side of the field and along the edge of Black Plantation for 100 yards before walking across it to a stile. Continue to a white gate - to your right is Linthurst Farm. Keep to the righthand side of the field, by the fence to a stile. Then aim for the far lefthand corner of the field where there is a stile and path sign and road. Turn right then left through a gate and walk along a grass track to a stile beside some trees and continue onto a gate close to All Saints church, Rangemore.

Newborough church.

38

Hoar Cross church.

NEWBOROUGH AND HOAR CROSS - 6 MILES

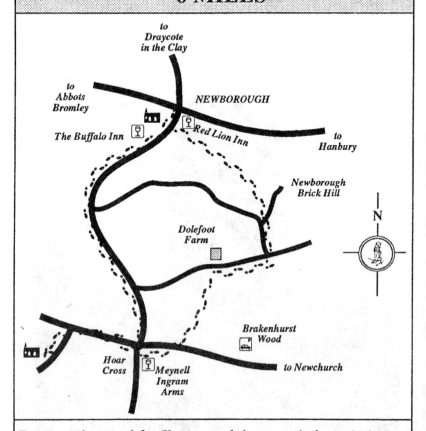

From opposite page - left. *(You can reach the same point by continuing over the bridge from Hoar Cross and gaining the car park at Brakenhurst Wood, turn left along the track and follow it down to Coal Hill and track. Continue ahead on this to the lane.)* In 100 yards the lane forks and take the lefthand one and in a few yards is a stile and path sign on your right. At first keep close to the field edge on your right before bearing left over the large field to reach a stile and views to Newborough. Continue ahead to the righthand hedge to a gate. Bear right and cross the field to a stile and path sign. Turn left to return to the centre of Newborough.

HOAR CROSS - The hall was formerly the home of the Meynell Ingrams. The church- known as the Cathedral of the Midlands - dates from the 19th century and was designed by George Frederick Bodley, who designed Liverpool Cathedral; there are many similarities. The central tower is 110 feet high.

NEWBOROUGH AND HOAR CROSS
- 6 MILES
- allow 2 to 3 hours.

➡ *Newborough - Hoar Cross - Hoar Cross Church - Hoar Cross - Brakenhurst Wood - Dolefoot Farm - Newborough Brick Hill - Newborough.*

- *O.S. 1:25,000 Pathfinder Series Sheet No.02/12 - Abbots Bromley.*

- *Roadside parking in Newborough. Car park at entrance to Brakenhurst Wood. Grid Ref. SK139233.*

- *Red Lion Inn, The Buffalo Inn, Newborough. Meynell Ingram Arms, Hoar Cross.*

ABOUT THE WALK - Newborough and Hoar Cross are situated in delightful countryside, rich in history. Newborough dresses in wells each May Day Bank Holiday. Hoar Cross is an amazing church in a secluded location and there are pleasant walks in Brakenhurst wood. Combined they make rewarding walking but alas the footpaths/rights of way are a disaster! I have never experienced so much trouble. The path signs are there but you cannot get through the hedges, as a result you have to do a lot of road walking. Thankfully they are quiet roads and because the area deserves exploring, I have included it in this book.

WALKING INSTRUCTIONS - From the centre of Newborough walk southwards on the Hoar Cross road, passing the Red Lion Inn and Buffalo Inn. Ignore the path signs for you cannot get through! It is 1 1/2 miles to Hoar Cross and the Meynell Ingram Arms. Turn right at the cross roads and ascend the road past Brakenhurst Farm and take the road to your right, aiming for Hoar Cross church. Retrace your steps back to Hoar Cross and cross the road following the Newchurch road. Just before the bridge over the stream (a subsidiary of the River Swarbourn) turn left through the stile. Keep to the righthand edge of the field beside Brakenhurst Wood on your right to a gap in the field boundary. Here leave the wood and aim for the lefthand corner of the field ahead. Keep to the righthand side of it to reach a gate, path sign and road beside Dolefoot Farm. Turn right along the lane and in 1/4 mile turn left along the lane on your

BURTON UPON TRENT
- 4 1/2 MILES

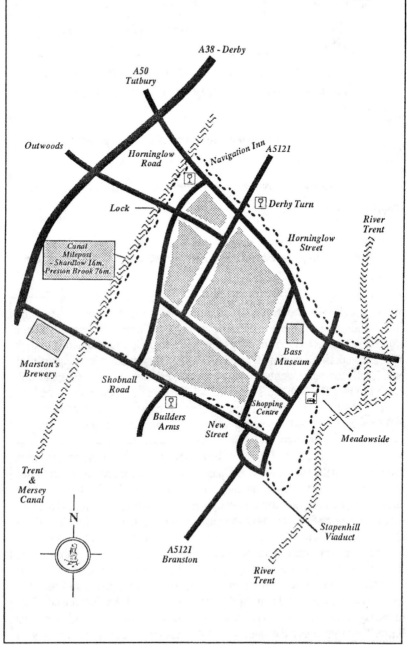

BURTON UPON TRENT
- 4 1/2 MILES
- allow 2 hours or more.

➡ *Central Burton Upon Trent - Shobnall - Trent & Mersey Canal - Horninglow - Bass Museum - River Trent - Trent Washlands Park - Central Burton Upon Trent.*

 O.S. 1:25,000 Pathfinder Series Sheet No. SK 22/32 - Burton Upon Trent.

- The walk starts from the car park on Meadowside, but there are others adjoining the route on Green Street and just off New Street.

Leopard Inn, Dog Inn, Black Horse Inn, Navigation Inn, Victoria Inn, Derby Turn Inn, Burton Upon Trent.

ABOUT THE WALK - Although based on Burton Upon Trent and walking some of its roads the walk will come as a surprise, for the area is extremely attractive, with several magnificent buildings, a delightful park with a 'trim trail', and, being a brewery town an impressive brewery museum and of course, numerous Inns. To complete the picture you follow a very pleasant stretch of the Trent & Mersey Canal. There is enough to see and do here to occupy an afternoon while walking a few miles!

WALKING INSTRUCTIONS - From the car park on Meadowside, near The Library, walk away from the town - westwards - to gain a tarmaced path and the Andresey Bridge, built in 1884, over the River Trent. Bear right on the path after crossing the bridge and enter the Washlands Park, around which is a 'trim trail'. You soon walk through a children's play area and keep on the path nearest the river with the remains of an Abbey on the other side. On your left is a rugby field. In about 1/4 miles gain the walkway - Stapenhill Viaduct - and turn right along it towards the town. Keep straight ahead along Fleet Street - there is a car park on your left - and just ahead is B & Q. In front of it turn right along Abbey Street and at the end pass the 19th century London designed Leopard Inn. Continue ahead on Lichfield Street, passing the Dog Inn. Turn left along New Street - on your right is the entrance to the Burton Shopping Centre. For the next mile you keep straight ahead, first on New Street, then Moor Street and passing under the railway line, and along Shobnall Road. Upon reaching the Canal bridge - No. 33, turn left down onto the towpath with Shobnall Marina on your left. Turn right along the towpath and pass under the bridge.

Keep on the towpath for the next mile passing canal milepost - Shardlow 16 miles/Preston Brook 76 miles. Next pass a lock, and a 1/3 mile later approach Horninglow and the Navigation Inn on your right. Leave the canal here and ascend to Horninglow Road. Turn right along the road, and for the next 1 1/2 mile to the River Trent you keep straight ahead at all road junctions. First along Horninglow Road. Pass the Derby Turn Inn and continue along Horninglow Street, passing over the railway lines, and in a 1/3 mile pass the impressive Magistrates Court on your left and reach the Bass Museum on your right. Continue ahead on Bridge Street and just before the River Trent, on your right, is Nunneley House - built in c.1760 by Samuel Sketchley, a brewer. Later it was occupied by Joseph Nunneley's Brewery. Just after the building turn right down the gradient path to regain Meadowside and car park. The tarmaced path leads round the building to the Andresey Bridge over the River Trent.

BURTON UPON TRENT - The town is synonymous with brewing but it was the monks at The Abbey founded in 1004 who discovered the local water was particularly suited to brewing. It wasn't until the 18th century that Burton brewing became more universally well known as they could export their produce along the canal to the sea ports. In 1880 there were about 40 breweries in the town. Over the last century they have amalgamated or been taken over, and today there are just the three universally known names.

Trent & Mersey Canal at Horninglow.

THIS BRIDGE AND VIADUCT
WERE PRESENTED TO THE BOROUGH OF BURTON UPON TRENT
BY THE RIGHT HONOURABLE MICHAEL ARTHUR BARON BURTON
AND THE BRIDGE WAS DECLARED FREE OF TOLL BY THE CORPORATION
ON THE THIRTEENTH DAY OF APRIL 1898

Stapenhill Viaduct.

BRANSTON - 6 MILES

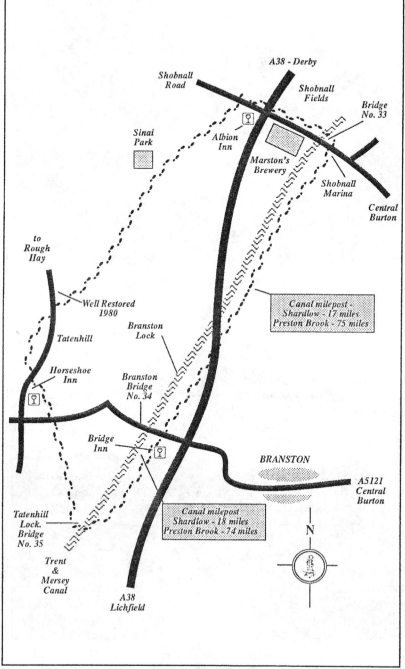

A38 - Derby

Shobnall Road

Shobnall Fields

Bridge No. 33

Sinai Park

Albion Inn

Marston's Brewery

Shobnall Marina

Central Burton

to Rough Hay

Well Restored 1980

Tatenhill

Branston Lock

Canal milepost -
Shardlow - 17 miles
Preston Brook - 75 miles

Horseshoe Inn

Branston Bridge No. 34

Bridge Inn

BRANSTON

A5121 Central Burton

N

Tatenhill Lock. Bridge No. 35

Canal milepost
Shardlow - 18 miles
Preston Brook - 74 miles

Trent & Mersey Canal

A38 Lichfield

BRANSTON
- 6 MILES
- allow 3 or more hours.

⇢ *Branston Bridge - Trent & Mersey Canal - Tatenhill Lock -Yews Bridge - Tatenhill - Prince's Covert - Sinai Park - Shobnall - Trent & Mersey Canal - Branston Bridge.*

- O.S. 1:25,000 Pathfinder Series - Sheet No SK 22/32 - Burton Upon Trent.

No official one, but roadside parking at Branston Bridge.

- Horseshoe Inn, Tatenhill. Albion Inn, Shobnall. Bridge Inn.

ABOUT THE WALK - A stunning walk; first beside the canal to the impressive Tatenhill Lock - cover photograph. Here you leave the canal to gain Tatenhill village, with an Inn and Hall. A short but steady ascent brings you onto the ridge of Battlestead Hill, providing superlative views over Burton Upon Trent and the canal below. You follow the ridge to Sinai Park and its remarkable timber framed and moated building. From here you descend to Shobnall and walk along the road to the canal. Two miles of walking beside it passing Branston Lock returns you to Branston Bridge, and the perfectly sited canal pub, the Bridge Inn. Quite simply, a walk of exceptional character.

WALKING INSTRUCTIONS - From Branston Bridge, walk towards the inn and descend the path on the right of it to the canal. Keep ahead beside the canal on your right and pass canal milepost - Shardlow 18 miles / Preston Brook 74 miles. Little over 1/2 mile later gain Tatenhill Lock - bridge No.35. Ascend and turn right over the canal and follow the well defined path along the field edge on your right. Keep the field edge on your right all the way, as the path becomes a track which is well stiled and gated. A mile from the canal gain the road at Yews Bridge. Bear right to the fenced path and continue with a rock face on your right to a stile. Cross an open field to another stile and bear left up the track to the road in Tatenhill. On your left is the village stores and Horseshoe Inn.

Turn right along the road past the Church, dedicated to St. Michael's & All

Angels, and the impressive hall just afterwards. 150 yards later, and just before a well restored in 1980, turn right. The path along the track leads to the woodland of Battlestead Hill. Don't follow this but ascend the field and at the top head for the righthand corner of the field to the wooden stile. Ascend this and keep the field edge on your right. Soon pass a stile on your right, but don't use it. Continue along the field edge to a stile. Shortly afterwards turn right over a stile and keep the field edge on your left as you walk along the crest of the ridge towards Sinai Park, 1/2 mile away. Pass the farm well to the right to a stile. Continue slightly to your left to pass a very impressive moated timber framed house and shortly afterwards gain the farm road. Follow it to a solitary house on your right. Just after it continue ahead, descend the field and regain the road and follow it to Shobnall Road, opposite the Post Office. Turn right along the road for 1/2 mile, passing under the A38 road and past Marston's Brewery. At the canal bridge, turn right and descend to the towpath and keep the canal on your right for the next two miles back to Branston Bridge. On the way passing milepost - Shardlow 17 miles / Preston Brook 75 miles, and Branston Lock.

BRANSTON - Gave its name to the famous pickle although it is not made here. Sinai Park was the summer residence of the Burton Abbey monks. The moated timber framed building dates from the 15th century.

TATENHILL LOCK
J.J.CREBER

48

Remember and observe the Country Code

 Enjoy the countryside and respect its life and work.

 Guard against all risk of fire.

 Fasten all gates.

 Keep your dogs under close control.

 Keep to public paths across farmland.

 Use gates and stiles to cross fences, hedges and walls.

 Leave livestock, crops and machinery alone.

 Take your litter home - pack it in; pack it out.

 Help to keep all water clean.

 Protect wildlife, plants and trees.

 Take special care on country roads

 Make no unnecessary noise.

EQUIPMENT NOTES
.. some personal thoughts from John N. Merrill

BOOTS - *For summer use and day walking I wear lightweight boots. For high mountains and longer trips I prefer a good quality boot with a full leather upper, of medium weight, with a vibram sole. I always add a foam cushioned insole to help cushion the base of my feet.*

SOCKS - *I generally wear two thick pairs as this helps minimise blisters. The inner pair are of loop stitch variety and approximately 80% wool. - Thorlo socks are excellent. The outer are a thick rib pair of approximately 80% wool.*

WATERPROOFS - *for general walking I wear a T shirt or cotton shirt with a cotton wind jacket on top. You generate heat as you walk and I prefer to layer my clothes to avoid getting too hot. Depending on the season will dictate how many layers you wear. In soft rain I just use my wind jacket for I know it quickly dries out. In heavy or consistant rain I slip on a neoprene lined cagoule, and although hot and clammy it does keep me reasonably dry. Only in extreme conditions will I don overtrousers, much preferring to get wet and feel comfortable. I never wear gaiters!*

FOOD - *as I walk I carry bars of chocolate, for they provide instant energy and are light to carry. In winter a flask of hot coffee is welcome. I never carry water and find no hardship from not doing so, but this is a personal matter! From experience I find the more I drink the more I want and sweat. You should always carry some extra food such as trail mix & candy bars etc., for emergencies.*

RUCKSACKS - *for day walking I use a climbing rucksack of about 40 litre capacity and although it leaves excess space it does mean that the sac is well padded, with an internal frame and padded shoulder straps. Inside apart from the basics for one day in winter I carry gloves, balaclava, spare pullover and a pair of socks.*

MAP & COMPASS - *when I am walking I always have the relevant map - preferably 1:25,000 scale - open in my hand. This enables me to constantly check that I am walking the right way. In case of bad weather I carry a compass, which once mastered gives you complete confidence in thick cloud or mist.*

WALK RECORD CHART

Date walked -

Okeover Park - 5 1/2 miles ....

Stanton & The Weaver Hills - 6 miles ....

Hollington & Croxden Abbey - 3 miles ....

Rocester & River Dove - 5 1/2 miles ....

Calwich Abbey and River Dove - 4 1/2 miles ....

Kingstone - 4 miles ....

Bagot's Park - 5 miles ....

Tutbury & Hanbury - 7 miles ....

Hanbury & Coton in the Clay - 2 miles ....

Hanbury, Fauld Crater & Greaves Wood - 5 1/2 miles ....

Blithfield Reservoir - 6 miles ....

Needwood Forest - 7 1/2 miles ....

Newborough and Hoar Cross - 6 miles ....

Burton Upon Trent - 4 1/2 miles ....

Branston - 6 miles ....

THE JOHN MERRILL WALK BADGE

Complete six of the walks in this book and get the above special embroidered badge and signed certificate. Badges are black cloth with lettering and walking man ered in four colours and measure 3 1/2" diameter.

(BADGE ORDER FORM)

Date and details of walk - completed...

....

NAME ....

ADDRESS ....

....

Price: £3.00 each including postage, VAT and signed completion certificate.
Amount enclosed (Payable to El Morro Equipment Ltd) ..

**From: El Morro Equipment Ltd.,
19, Moseley Street, Ripley,
Derbyshire. DE5 3DA**

✆ /**Fax** (01773) - 512143

********** *YOU MAY PHOTOCOPY THIS FORM* ***********

"I'VE DONE A JOHN MERRILL WALK" T SHIRT

- Green with white lettering and walking man logo.
Send £7.50 to El Morro Equipment Ltd., stating size required.
John Merrill's "Happy Walking!" Cap - £3.00

"From footprint to finished book"

THE SNOWDON CHALLENGE
CHARNWOOD FOREST CHALLENGE WALK
THREE COUNTIES CHALLENGE WALK (Peak District).
CAL-DER-WENT WALK by Geoffrey Carr,
THE QUANTOCK WAY
THE CARNEDDAU CHALLENGE WALK
THE BELVOIR WITCHES CHALLENGE WALK.
THE SWEET PEA CHALLENGE WALK
THE MIDDLEWICH CHALLENGE WALK
THE SALT & SAILS TRAIL by David Burkill-Howarth

INSTRUCTION & RECORD -
HIKE TO BE FIT.....STROLLING WITH JOHN
THE JOHN MERRILL WALK RECORD BOOK

MULTIPLE DAY WALKS -
THE RIVERS'S WAY
PEAK DISTRICT: HIGH LEVEL ROUTE
PEAK DISTRICT MARATHONS
THE LIMEY WAY
THE PEAKLAND WAY

COAST WALKS & NATIONAL TRAILS -
ISLE OF WIGHT COAST PATH
PEMBROKESHIRE COAST PATH
THE CLEVELAND WAY
WALKING ANGELSEY'S COASTLINE.
WALKING THE ISLE OF MAN COASTAL PATH

CYCLING Compiled by Arnold Robinson.
CYCLING AROUND THE NORTH YORK MOORS.
CYCLING AROUND MATLOCK.
CYCLING AROUND CASTLETON & the Hope Valley.
CYCLING AROUND CHESTERFIELD.
CYCLING IN THE YORKSHIRE WOLDS.
CYCLING AROUND LEICESTERSHIRE & RUTLAND
CYCLING AROUND BUXTON.
CYCLING AROUND LINCOLNSHIRE
CYCLING AROUND STAFFORDSHIRE
CYCLING AROUND THE LAKE DISTRICT
CYCLING AROUND DERBY
CYCLING AROUND THE ISLE OF MAN
CYCLING AROUND THE COTSWOLDS
CYCLING AROUND NORTHUMBRIA
"PEAK DISTRICT CYCLING - Round the bend with Graham." by G.Kirkby

PEAK DISTRICT HISTORICAL GUIDES -
A to Z GUIDE OF THE PEAK DISTRICT
DERBYSHIRE INNS - an A to Z guide
HALLS AND CASTLES OF THE PEAK DISTRICT & DERBYSHIRE
TOURING THE PEAK DISTRICT & DERBYSHIRE BY CAR
DERBYSHIRE FOLKLORE
PUNISHMENT IN DERBYSHIRE
CUSTOMS OF THE PEAK DISTRICT & DERBYSHIRE
WINSTER - a souvenir guide
ARKWRIGHT OF CROMFORD
LEGENDS OF DERBYSHIRE
DERBYSHIRE FACTS & RECORDS
TALES FROM THE MINES by Geoffrey Carr
FURTHER TALES FROM THE MNINES by Geoffrey Carr
PEAK DISTRICT PLACE NAMES by Martin Spray
PEAK DISTRICT MONSTERS by Alan Smith
HERNE'S CHILDREN - Part Two of the Peakland Trilogy - "Herne's Champions" by Peter E. Noon

JOHN MERRILL'S MAJOR WALKS -
TURN RIGHT AT LAND'S END
WITH MUSTARD ON MY BACK
TURN RIGHT AT DEATH VALLEY
EMERALD COAST WALK

SKETCH BOOKS -
SKETCHES OF THE PEAK DISTRICT

COLOUR BOOK:-
THE PEAK DISTRICT.......something to remember her by.

OVERSEAS GUIDES -
HIKING IN NEW MEXICO - Vol I - The Sandia and Manzano Mountains.
Vol 2 - Hiking "Billy the Kid" Country. Vol 4 - N.W. area - "Hiking Indian Country."
"WALKING IN DRACULA COUNTRY" - Romania.

VISITOR'S GUIDES - MATLOCK. BAKEWELL. ASHBOURNE.

NEW
BUTTON BADGES

- 58m.m. diameter
all at 30p each
- postage & packing 1 to 5 - 30p.

6 to 12 60p. 20 or more £1.00

	Quantity
JOHN MERRILL HAPPY WALKING BADGE	
FOOTSLOGGER BADGE	
WORLD'S SPEEDIEST HIKER	
WORLD'S DRIEST BOGTROTTER	
WORLD'S MOST CONFIDENT CLIMBER	
WORLD'S SLIMMEST BACKPACKER	
WORLD'S LEADING FELL RUNNER	
WORLD'S TIDIEST CAMPER	
WORLD'S LIGHTEST BACKPACKER	
WORLD'S HIGHEST OVERNIGHT CAMP	
DON'T FOLLOW ME - I'M LOST!	
I GOT WET IN THE PEAK DISTRICT	
IT WAS WINDY ON THE SUMMIT!	
GO CLIMB AN EDGE - PEAK DISTRICT	
FISHERMAN - TALL STORIES!	
FISHERMAN - THE ONE THAT GOT AWAY!	
WORLD'S WOBBLIEST CYCLIST	
ITS QUICKER BY BIKE!	
All have title with a humerous sketch.	

Name..

Address ....

....

Amount enclosed payable to El Morro Equipment Ltd. ....
19, Moseley Street, Ripley, Derbyshire. DE5 3DA

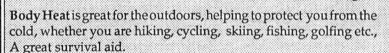